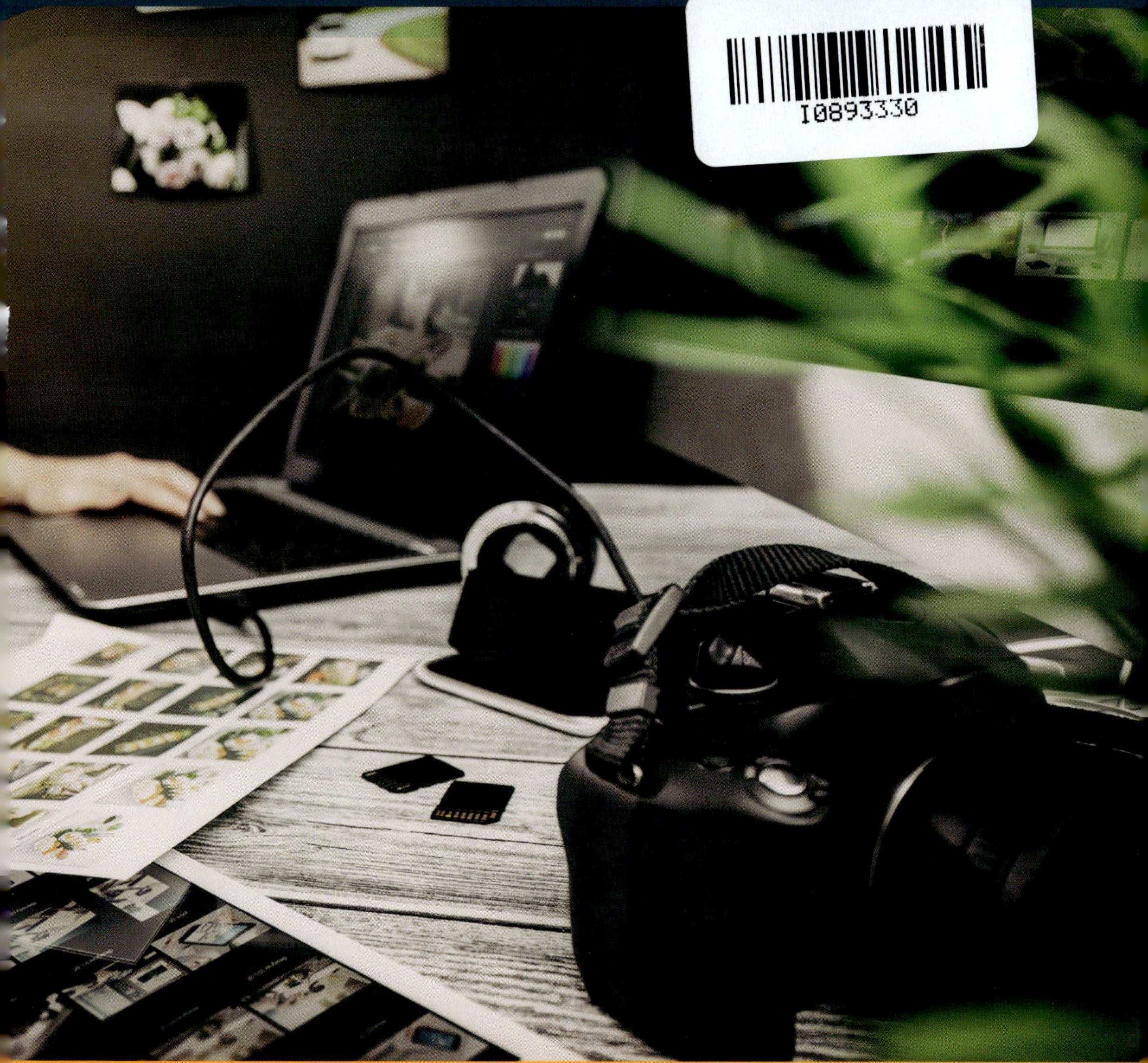

THE 12 BIGGEST BREAKTHROUGHS IN PHOTO TECHNOLOGY

by Allan Morey

12 STORY LIBRARY

www.12StoryLibrary.com

12-Story Library is an imprint of Bookstaves.

Photographs ©: scyther5/iStockphoto, cover, 1; Hajotthu/CC3.0, 4; Gemma Frisius/PD, 4; PD, 5; McAllister/PD, 5; PD, 6; Joseph Nicéphore Niépce/PD, 7; Liudmila & Nelson/PD, 8; Susanna Celeste Castelli, DensityDesign Research Lab/CC4.0, 8; Everett Historical/Shutterstock.com, 9; Nicolaas Henneman/CCO, 10; Everett Historical/Shutterstock.com, 11; Walker Art Library/Alamy Stock Photo, 12; Wellcome Images/CC4.0, 12; Wellcome Images/CC4.0, 13; Everett Historical/Shutterstock.com, 13; Science & Society Picture Library/Getty Images, 14; Daily Herald Archive/SSPL/Getty Images, 15; Everett Historical/Shutterstock.com, 16; Albert Tissandier/PD, 17; Kodak/PD, 17; PD, 18; Lenscap Photography/Shutterstock.com, 19; Mr. Gray/PD, 20; Morio/CC3.0, 21; Library of Congress, 22; © www.wright-brothers.com, 22; NASA/EAS/STScl/J Hester and P Scowen (Arizona State University), 23; Dnalor 01/CC3.0, 24; Denis Botarev/Shutterstock.com, 25; shutterlk/Shutterstock.com, 26; Syda Productions/Shutterstock.com, 27; Eugene Ilchenko/CC2.0, 28; B. C. Forbes Publishing Co./PD, 29; S Photos/Shutterstock.com, 29

ISBN
978-1-63235-585-0 (hardcover)
978-1-63235-639-0 (paperback)
978-1-63235-699-4 (ebook)

Library of Congress Control Number: 2018940544

Printed in the United States of America
Mankato, MN
July 2018

Table of Contents

1

The Camera Obscura Turns the World Upside Down

No one knows when people first noticed a strange optical illusion. When light from the sun shines through a small hole and into a darkened room, it creates an image. The image appears on the wall opposite the hole. It shows the scene outside the room.

The image is upside down. That is because light travels in a straight line. Light from the bottom of the outdoor scene shines up through the hole to the top of the wall. Light from the top of the scene travels down through the hole to the bottom of the wall. This image became known as camera obscura. These are the Latin words for dark room.

By the early 1500s, people were building box-size devices called camera obscuras. But the images these made were not very clear.

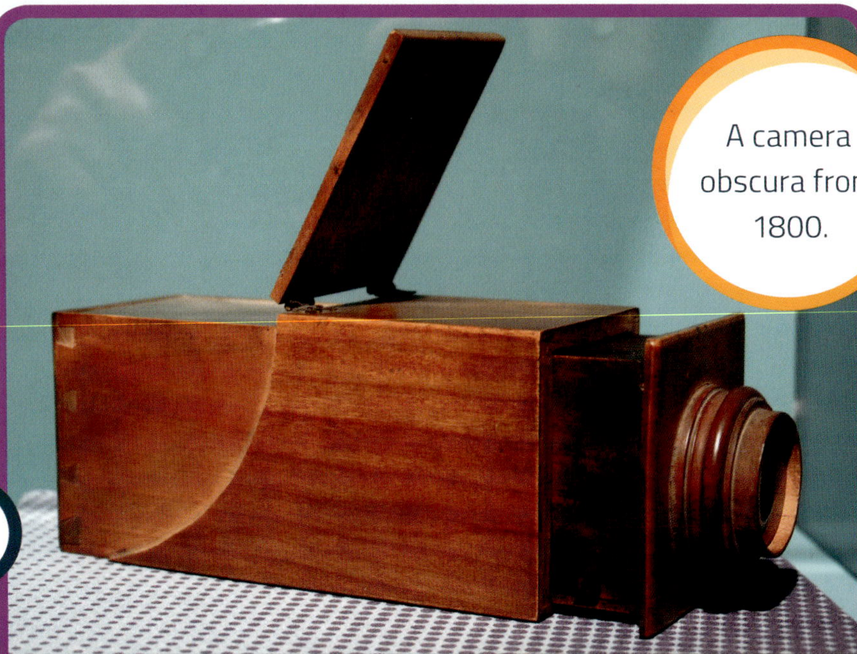

A camera obscura from 1800.

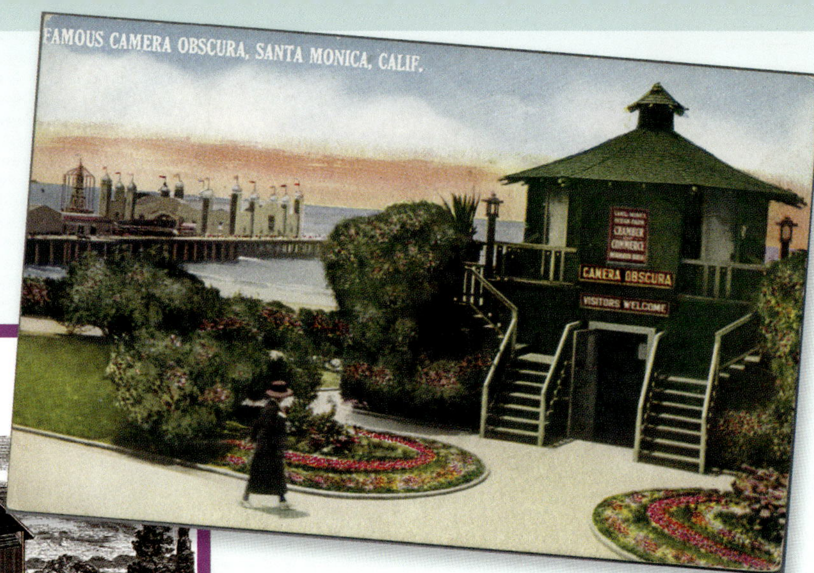

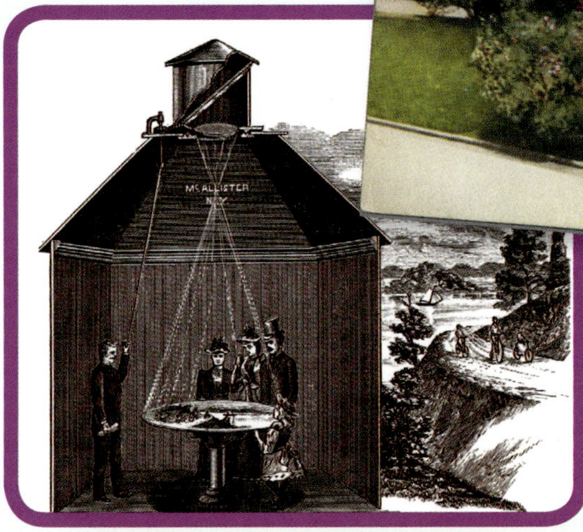

400 BCE

Year a Chinese philosopher named Mozi wrote about a camera obscura image. This was the first recorded mention.

- Camera obscura is the Latin phrase for dark room.
- Images from a camera obscura appear upside down.
- Camera obscuras were popular tourist attractions.

Italian scientist Daniel Barbaro placed a lens in the hole of a camera obscura. The image it created was much clearer and brighter. The image could be focused onto a surface, such as a sheet of paper. People could trace around it to make drawings or paintings.

In the late 1600s, German scientist Johann Zahn came up with more ideas to improve the camera obscura. For example, adding a mirror allowed the image to be projected. This type of camera obscura became popular in the 1800s. Large ones were built in coastal towns. They projected images of the seaside for tourists to view.

2

The First Photograph Is a View Out a Window

In the 1720s, German scientist Johann Heinrich Schulze did an important experiment. He proved that a chemical compound was photosensitive. When silver nitrate was exposed to sunlight, it turned dark.

In the late 1700s, British chemist Thomas Wedgwood made one of the first tries to take a photograph. He placed paper covered in silver nitrate in a camera obscura. All he got was a shadowy image.

In the early 1800s, French inventor Joseph-Nicéphore Niépce developed a new printing method. He called it heliography, or sun drawing. Niépce put bitumen, a tar-like substance, on a metal plate. Then he placed a drawing over the bitumen and set it in the sun. Sunlight shined through the lighter areas of the drawing and hardened some of the bitumen. Niépce washed away the rest of the bitumen. A negative of the drawing was left on the plate.

Niépce tried a similar process with a camera obscura. He aimed the camera out a window of his home in France. After eight hours of exposure, he took the metal plate out of the camera. He washed away the bitumen

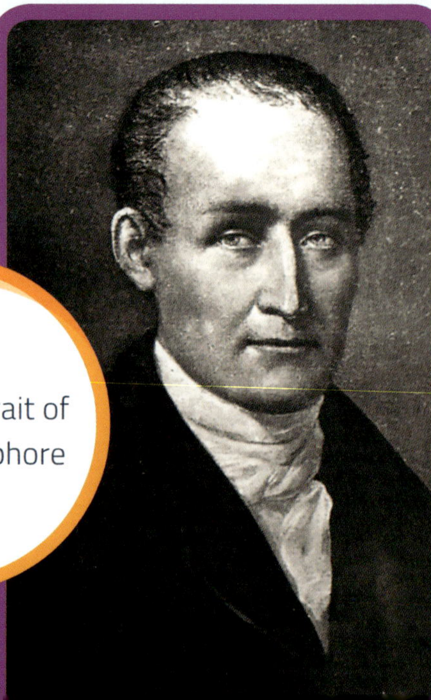

A 19th-century portrait of Joseph-Nicéphore Niépce.

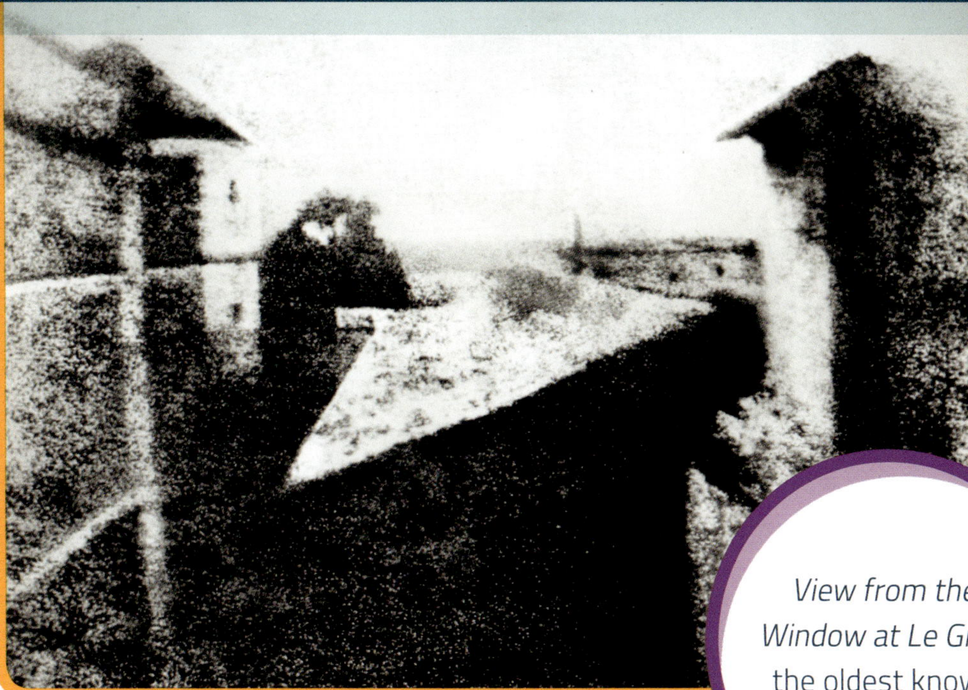

View from the Window at Le Gras, the oldest known photograph.

that didn't harden. What was left was a negative of the scene outside his window. From this plate, he printed the oldest known photograph. It is called *View from the Window at Le Gras.*

THE NEGATIVE IMAGE

Most early cameras produced a negative image. A negative looks the opposite of what is being photographed. Dark areas appear light, and light areas are dark. Printing or developing the negative to make a photograph reverses the dark and light areas.

1826

Approximate year Joseph-Nicéphore Niépce took the oldest known photograph.

- In the 1700s, scientists proved that sunlight discolors certain chemical compounds.
- The first photographs were taken using a camera obscura.
- They needed up to eight hours of exposure time.

3 Photography Takes Off with the Daguerreotype

Louis Daguerre was a French artist. He worked mostly on theater designs and sets. He also invented the diorama. A diorama is a three-dimensional scene. Daguerre's dioramas made audiences believe they were seeing real-life nature scenes.

Daguerre learned that a French inventor named Joseph-Nicéphore Niépce was making images with a simple camera called a camera obscura. Daguerre dreamed of capturing real-life scenes with photographs. Daguerre and Niépce started working together on a new photograph process.

Niépce died in 1833. But Daguerre went on with their research. He knew from Niépce's notes that

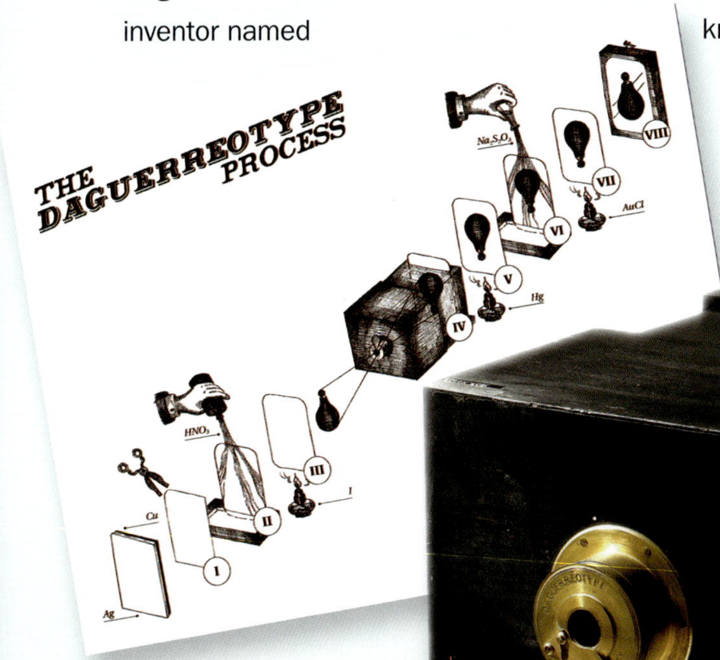

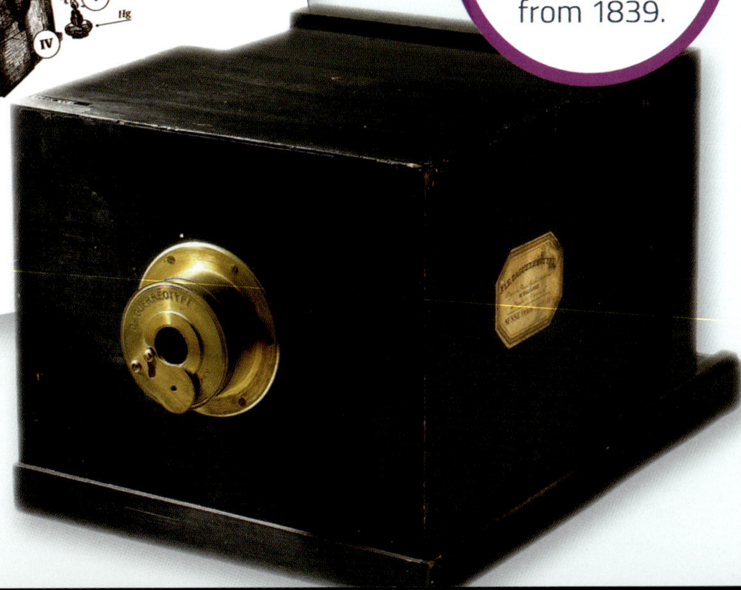

A daguerreotype camera from 1839.

sunlight could create an image on some surfaces that was not always visible right away. Daguerre just needed to find a way to make this latent image appear.

In 1835, Daguerre made a big discovery. He had a latent image on a copper plate. It was covered in a thin layer of silver. Daguerre exposed the plate to mercury vapor. The image appeared.

In 1837, Daguerre perfected his new photographic process. Creating an image took minutes of exposure time, not hours. The picture was clearer and much more detailed than Niépce's camera obscura had taken.

The photographs made with Daguerre's method were fragile. They were on thin metal plates. The plates were put behind glass to be protected and viewed. The images were one of a kind. They could not be copied.

Images made with Daguerre's process were called daguerreotypes. Studios soon opened to take people's portraits with this new method. Everybody wanted their portrait taken. The daguerreotype process was popular for many years.

3 million

Estimated number of daguerreotypes made in the United States in 1853.

- The daguerreotype is named for its inventor, Louis Daguerre.
- Daguerre first worked with Joseph-Nicéphore Niépce.
- A daguerreotype is a unique image on a thin copper plate coated with silver.

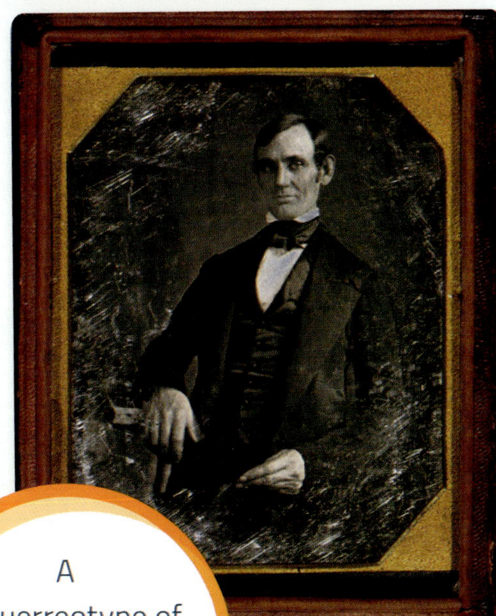

A daguerreotype of Abraham Lincoln taken between 1846-47.

4 Calotype Process Puts Images on Paper

Photographs called daguerreotypes were very popular. But they had many drawbacks. They were too expensive for many people. They were on thin metal plates and were easy to damage. The images could not be reproduced.

British inventor William Henry Fox Talbot looked for an alternative. He experimented with coating drawing paper with a salt solution. Then he soaked the paper in silver nitrate. This created photosensitive paper. He placed a plant on the paper and exposed the paper to sunlight. This process created a silhouetted image of the plant. But the image quickly faded.

Talbot tried capturing images with a camera obscura. Light shining through a camera obscura could create a negative image on his photosensitive paper. But like

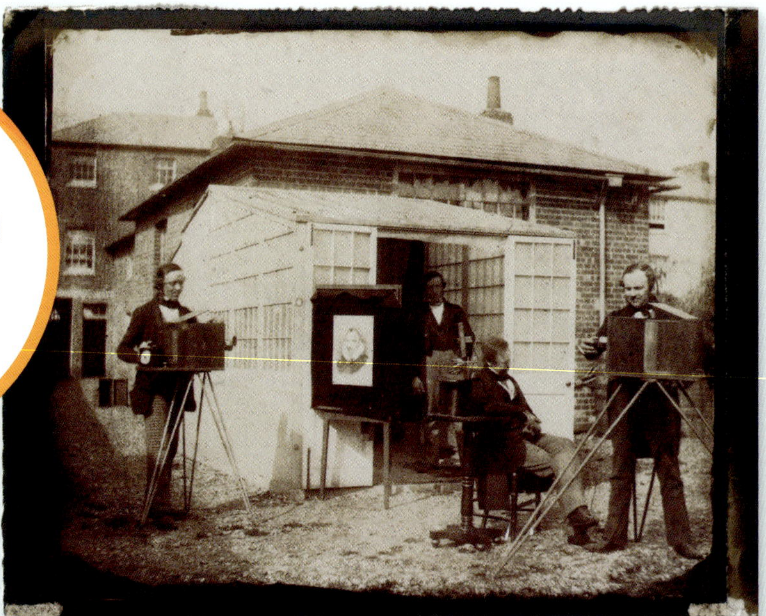

William Henry Fox Talbot (far right) demonstrating his calotype process in 1846.

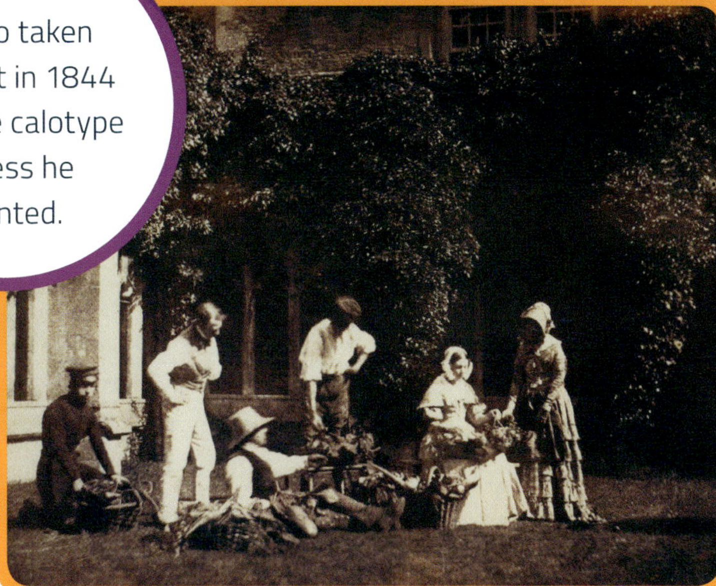

A photo taken by Talbot in 1844 using the calotype process he invented.

his earlier experiments, these images quickly faded.

Then Talbot had some help from British astronomer Sir John Herschel. Herschel developed what is called a fixing agent. This is a chemical compound that keeps an image from fading after exposure.

Talbot used Herschel's fixing agent on his images. He called his photographic process calotype. This comes from the Greek words for beautiful image. Thanks to Talbot, photographs could be produced as negatives. The negatives could be used to make copies.

THINK ABOUT IT

William Henry Fox Talbot was inspired to invent the calotype because he couldn't draw. He wanted a better way to make images of things he saw. Is it fair to use a camera to make art? Why or why not?

1841

Year William Henry Fox Talbot finalized his calotype process.

- Daguerreotypes were expensive and fragile.
- Calotypes were negatives on photosensitive paper.
- Many copies of an image could be produced from a calotype.

5 Wet-Collodion Process Speeds Up Exposure Time

In the mid-1800s, British artist Frederick Scott Archer developed a new photographic process. He used a liquid mixture called collodion.

Collodion was made using gun cotton. This is cotton soaked in nitric and sulfuric acids. The cotton was added to a mixture of ether and alcohol to make collodion. At the time, collodion was used for medical purposes. The syrupy liquid created a protective film when smeared over small wounds.

Archer's process started by covering a clear glass plate with collodion. Then the plate was treated with silver nitrate. While the plate was still wet, it was placed into a camera. Then a photograph was taken. It needed only seconds of exposure time. The plate needed to be developed

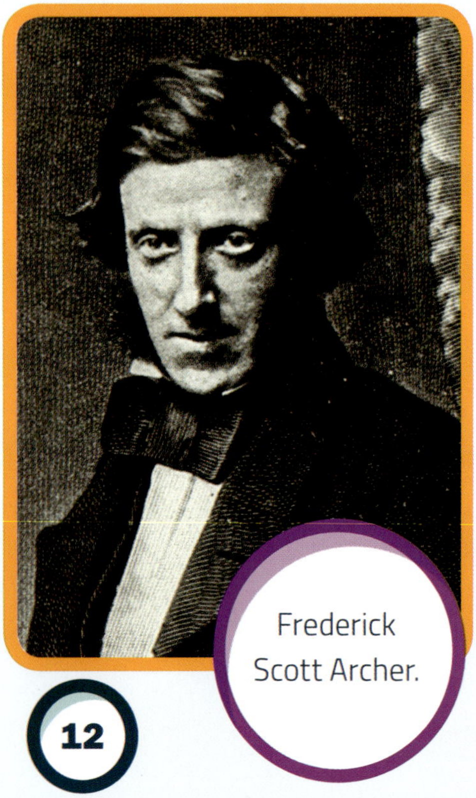

Frederick Scott Archer.

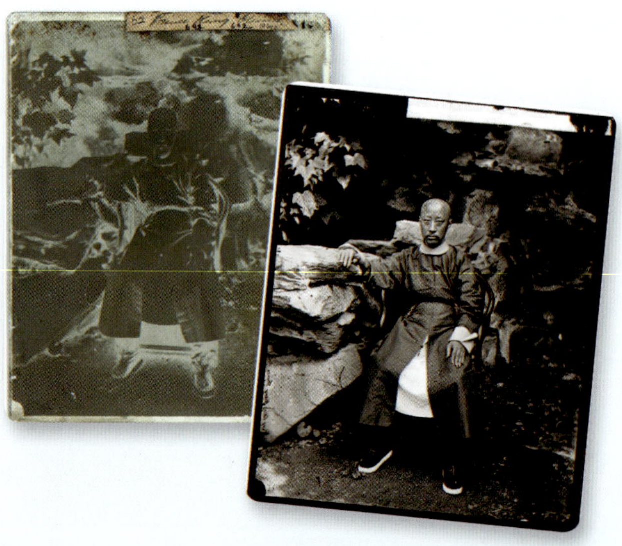

1851

Year Frederick Scott Archer invented the wet-collodion process.

- The wet-collodion process created detailed images, like the daguerreotype process.
- It created negatives, like the calotype process.
- The wet-collodion process only needed seconds of exposure time.

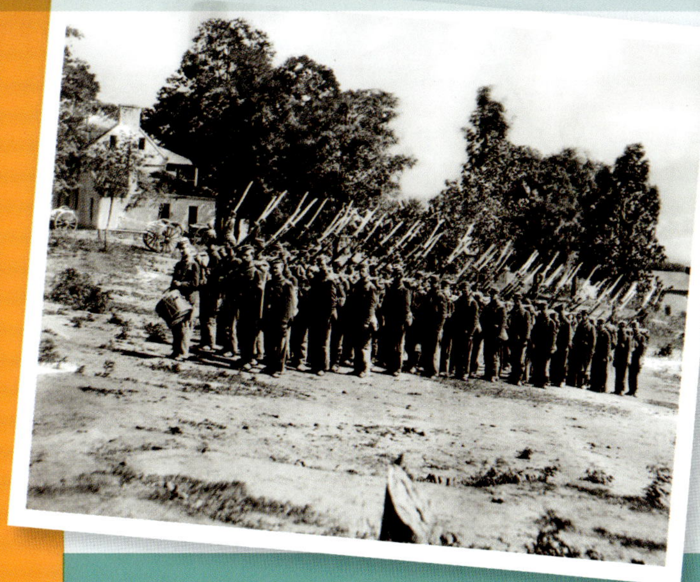

PHOTOGRAPHY ON THE BATTLEFIELD

American photographer Mathew Brady has been called the father of photojournalism. During the American Civil War, he hired a staff of about 20 photographers and sent them into war zones. Brady and his team took thousands of pictures of battlefields to document the war. They used Frederick Scott Archer's wet-collodion process to create their historic photographs.

right away, while it was still wet. And it needed to be done in a darkened room or tent.

The wet-collodion process was a big improvement over other photographic processes. Like a daguerreotype, it captured details. Like a calotype, it created a negative. Many copies of the image could be made. By the late 1800s, this was the most popular way to take photographs.

6

Dry Plates Are Easier and More Practical

From the mid-1850s until about 1881, making a photograph was hard. Photographs were taken using glass plates that were wet with harmful chemicals. They had to be developed right away, in the dark. The glass plates were easy to break.

In the 1850s, French doctor J.M. Taupenot tried something different. He poured albumen, made with egg whites, over a wet glass plate. He let it dry. Then he added a coating of silver nitrate. He let that dry, too. Taupenot created a new kind of photosensitive plate. It could be stored for weeks or months. It was easier to use, but it needed more exposure time.

Other scientists tried creating a dry-plate photographic process. British doctor Richard Leach Maddox came upon the best solution. He coated a glass plate with a gelatin emulsion made of acids and silver nitrate. He let it dry. Like Taupenot's plates, Maddox's plates were photosensitive. They could be stored for long periods. But their exposure times were much shorter.

The new dry plates had many advantages. They could be mass-produced. Photographers could buy them instead of having to prepare their own plates. Also, the short exposure time meant they could photograph moving objects.

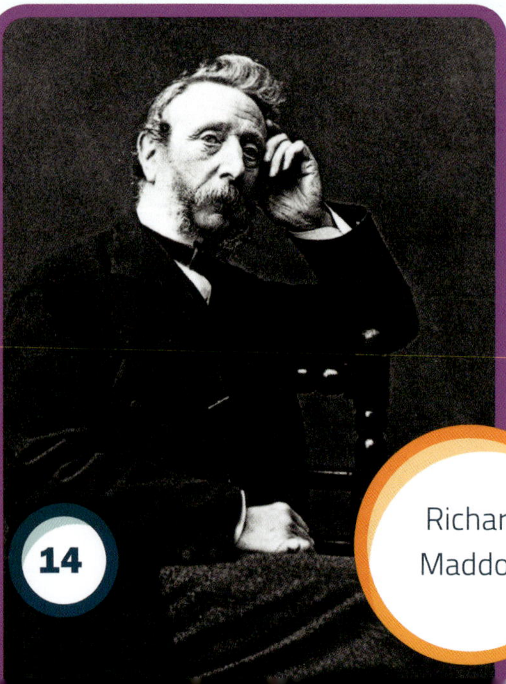

Richard Maddox.

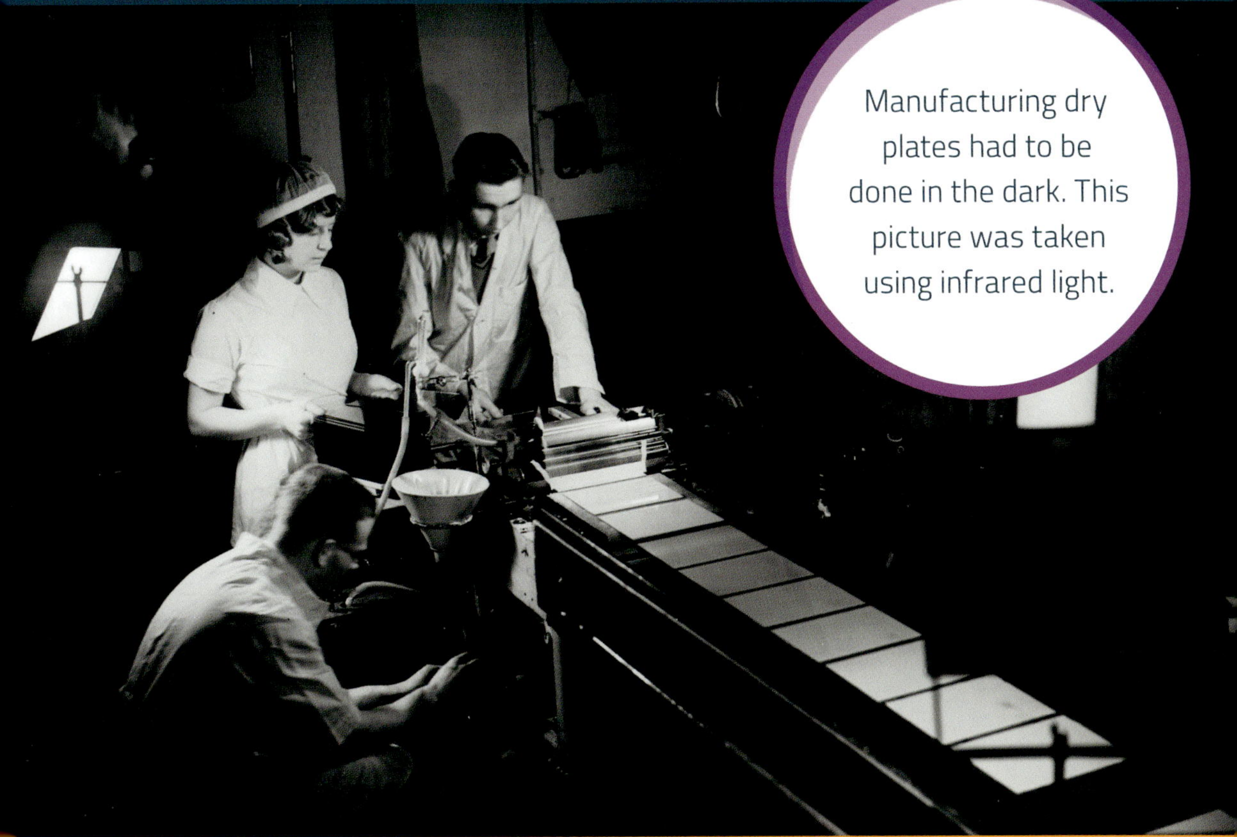

Manufacturing dry plates had to be done in the dark. This picture was taken using infrared light.

MAKING PHOTOGRAPHS WITH HONEY

In the mid-1800s, several people worked on a photographic process that used honey. After a plate was prepared, it was coated with honey. This kept the plate from drying for several days. It stayed photosensitive, but the honey doubled the exposure time.

1871

Year Robert Leach Maddox invented his dry-plate process.

- J.M. Taupenot used egg whites to make glass plates photosensitive.
- Dry plates could be stored for long periods of time.
- Using plates made with Richard Leach Maddox's process, photographers could capture moving objects.

7

Pictures Start to Move

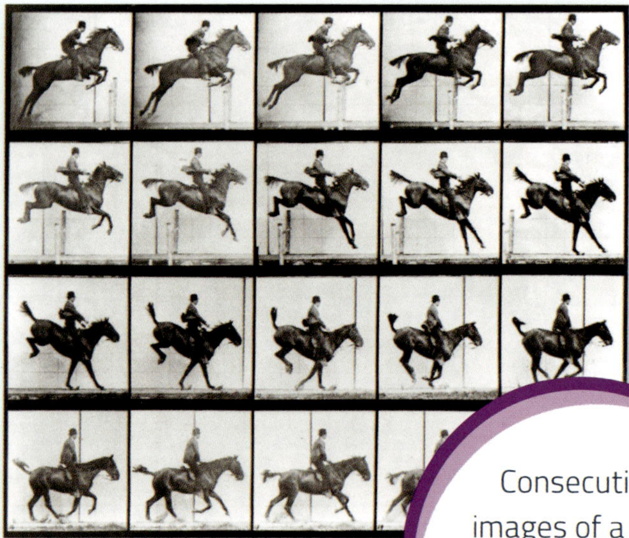

Consecutive images of a man riding a horse by Eadweard Muybridge in 1887.

In the late 1800s, English photographer Eadweard Muybridge took a series of photographs using many cameras. They showed people and animals in action. When the photos were viewed very quickly, one after another, the people and animals looked like they were moving.

Muybridge's work helped inspire the inventors of moving pictures. One was Thomas Edison. He and photographer William Kennedy Dickson built a working model of a motion picture camera. They called it a kinetograph. This camera took a series of photographs on a long strip of film. The film was viewed through a kinetoscope. This was a device with an eyepiece. When a series of photographs moved quickly through it, they gave the illusion of movement.

Edison is also credited with designing the perforated edges on film. They helped move film through a still camera. They kept movie film moving at a constant speed.

Today moving pictures, or movies, are one of the most popular forms of entertainment. People all over the world watch movies and TV shows on film.

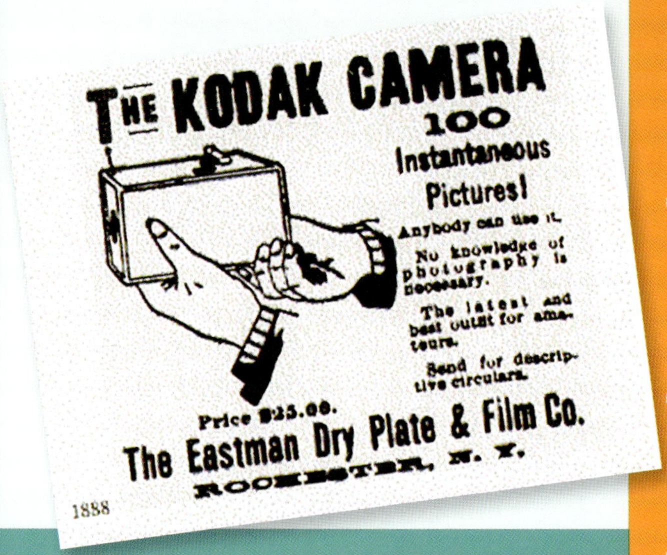

FLEXIBLE ROLL FILM

Early photographs were taken on glass plates or sheets of photosensitive paper. Cameras could only hold one at a time. Then, in the mid-1880s, inventor George Eastman began producing cameras that used a roll of paper film. People were able to take many photographs in a row.

1891

Year Thomas Edison patented the kinetograph.

- The idea for moving pictures probably came from photographers taking series of pictures of people and animals in action.
- Thomas Edison worked with William Kennedy Dickson to invent the kinetograph.
- The first movies were series of still photographs shown very quickly, one after another.

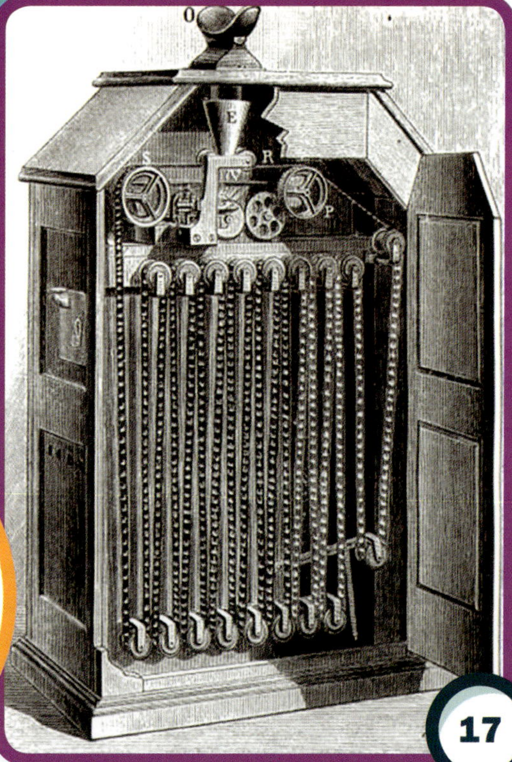

The inside of a kinetoscope showing how a moving strip of film gave the illusion of movement.

8 Photography Gets Colorful

For the first 100 years of photography, images were monochrome. They were black and white with shades of gray. Early photographic processes could only tell the difference between light and dark, not colors.

But people wanted color photographs. In the mid-1800s, things began to change. Some photographers tried using colored filters. They took several pictures of an image, using a different filter for each. Then they laid transparent prints on top of each other. They projected the layered image onto a screen. It looked like a color photograph.

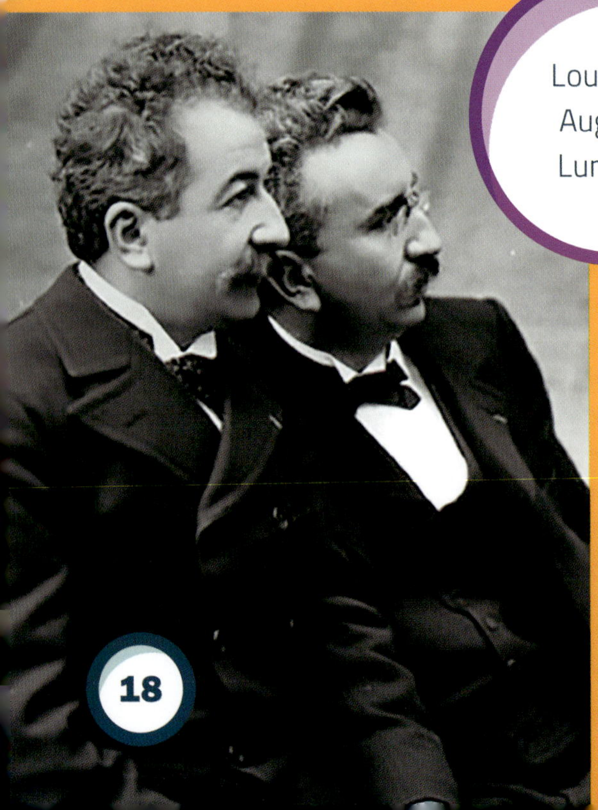

Louis and Auguste Lumière.

In the early 1900s, brothers Louis and Auguste Lumière made a surprising discovery. Potato starch had fine grains of red, blue, and green in it. Covering a glass plate with a wash of the starch created a kind of filter. A photosensitive liquid was added to the plate. When the plate was exposed to light, a color transparency was created. This could be used to make a color photograph. The new process was called Autochrome Lumière. It was

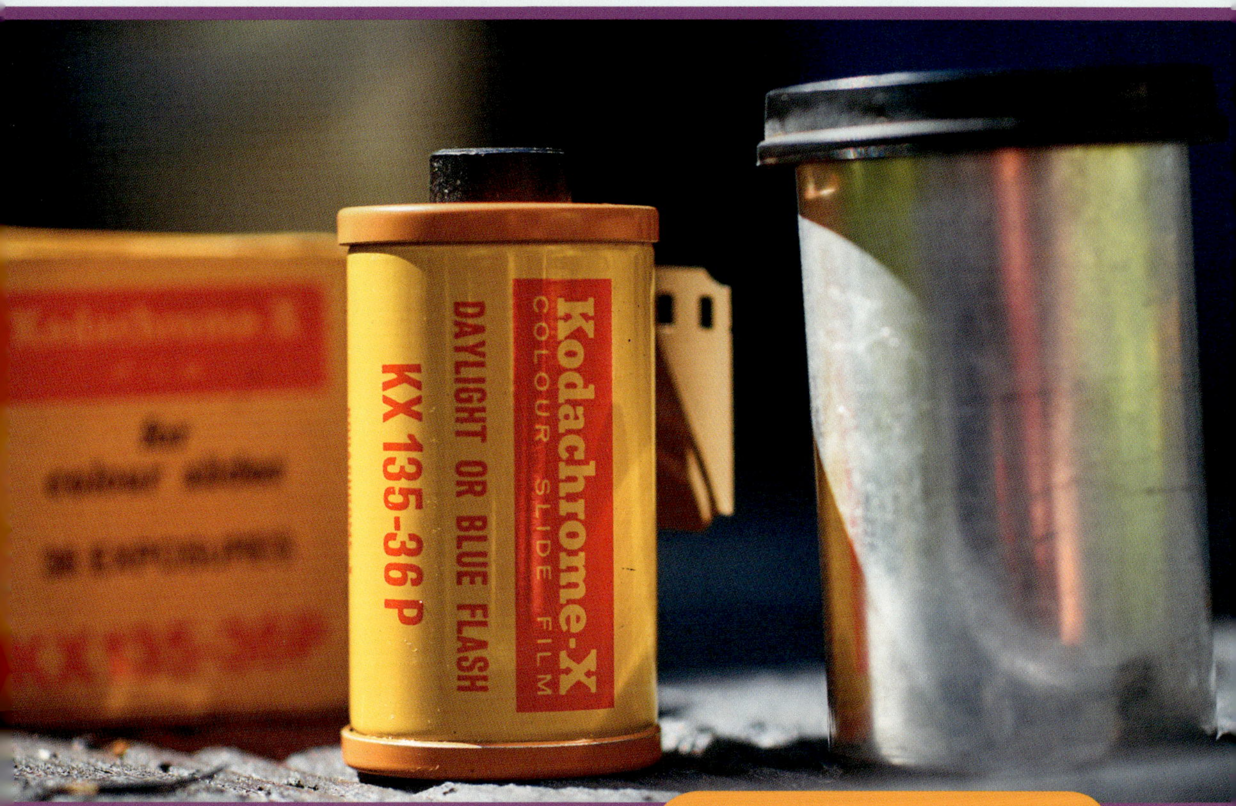

introduced in 1907 and used until the 1930s.

In 1935, the Eastman Kodak Company came out with Kodachrome film. It was very easy to use. People did not need to develop photographs themselves. They just took pictures and sent the film to Kodak to process. It was costly, but slowly color took over as the most popular type of photography. Today black-and-white photographs are usually taken only for artistic purposes.

$3.50

Cost of an early roll of 35mm Kodachrome film, or $30.67 in 2018 dollars.

- Some early color photographs were created with colored filters.
- Grains in potato starch made the first color photographs possible.
- Eastman Kodak's Kodachrome film made it easy to take color photographs.

9

Digital Cameras and Smartphones Make Everyone a Photographer

In the 1960s, scientists Willard E. Boyle and George E. Smith developed a new sensor. It was called a charge-coupled device, or CCD. It turned light into an electronic signal. In 1970, Boyle and Smith designed a video camera using their CCD sensor. Images from this device could be stored on a microchip instead of a roll of film.

2009

Year Willard Boyle and George Smith won the Nobel Prize in Physics for inventing the CCD sensor.

- The CCD sensor changed photography.
- Digital cameras had many features people wanted.
- Most people today take pictures with their smartphones.

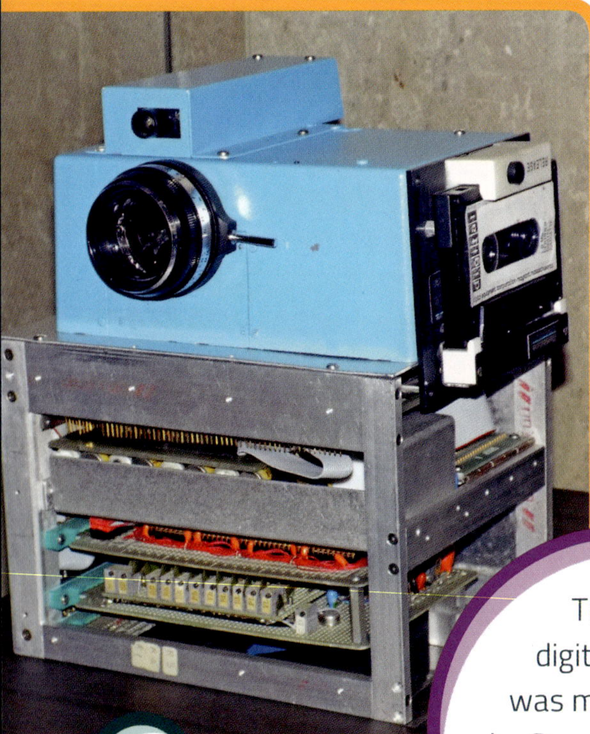

The first digital camera was made in 1975 by Steven Sasson, an engineer at Eastman Kodak.

Before long, this new technology was being used for photography. The first digital cameras were

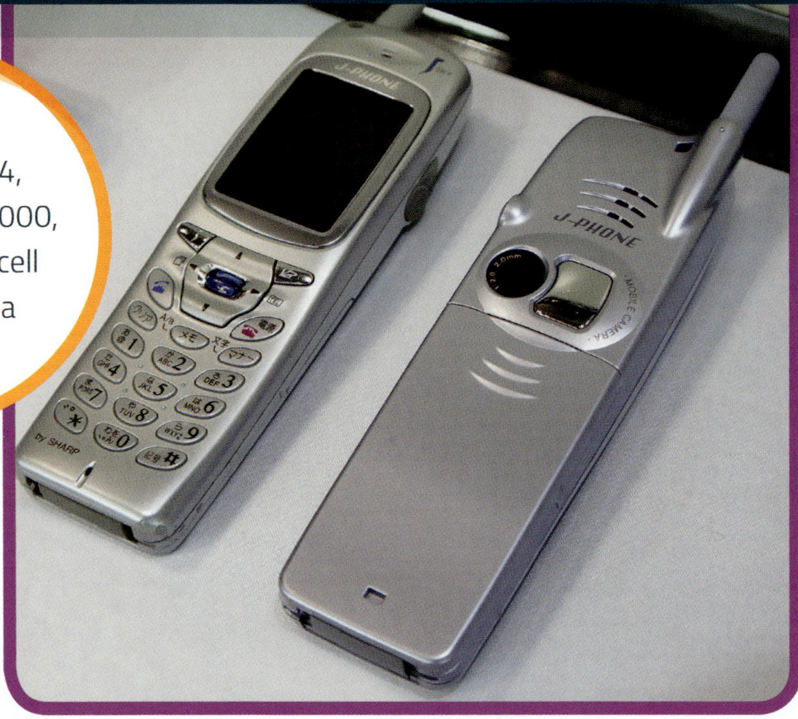

The Sharp J-SH04, introduced in 2000, was the first cell phone with a camera.

large, about the size of a toaster. They only took black-and-white photos. The images were stored on a cassette tape and needed a long exposure time. The images were not very clear.

Many advances were made in the 1980s. Digital cameras stored images on small memory chips. They didn't need to hold a roll of film. So camera companies could build small, handheld models. These were called point-and-shoot cameras. On earlier cameras, people had to adjust the lens to focus on an image. Digital cameras came with autofocus. New digital cameras took color photographs. They needed less exposure time. They could take quick bursts of photographs back-to-back. People could get shots of athletes and animals in action.

The first phones with built-in digital cameras became available in 2002. This completely changed how ordinary people took photographs. Once people started using smartphones, most ditched their cameras. Cameras in smartphones could take good photographs. These photographs were easy to upload to a computer or post on the internet.

10

Aerial Photography Takes Flight

Some of the earliest aerial photographs date from the American Civil War. Photographers rode up in hot air balloons to take pictures of enemy fortifications.

True aerial photography didn't start until after the Wright Brothers' first flight in 1903. Before long, aerial photography was being used for map making, military planning, and observing wildlife.

In 1946, the United States sent its first rocket into outer space. A camera on board took pictures of Earth. In 1957, the Soviet Union launched *Sputnik 1*, the first artificial satellite. Soon there were cameras in space.

Space cameras need to be very advanced. Their satellites zoom around Earth at incredible speeds. To keep images from blurring, exposure times are a thousandth of a second. The cameras must have very powerful lenses.

Cameras aboard satellites help scientists better understand the

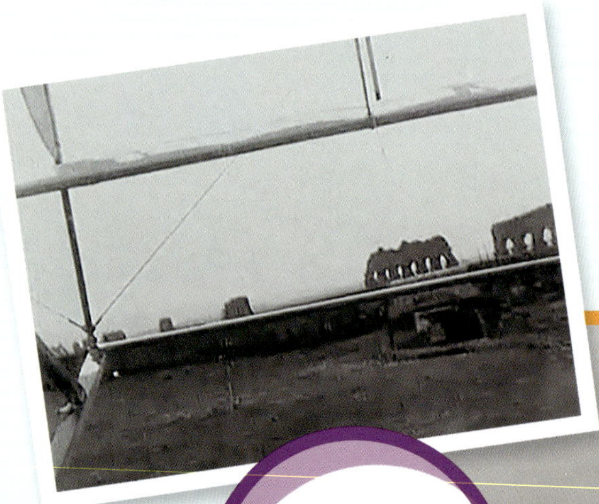

One of the first aerial photos.

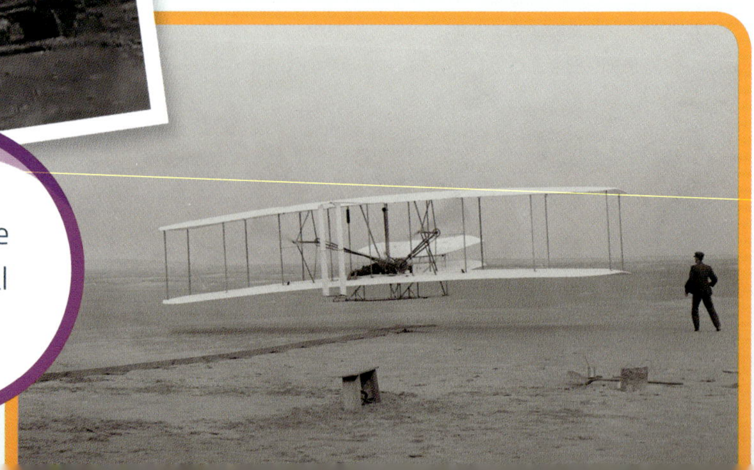

1909

Year the first photograph was taken from an airplane. Wilbur Wright was the pilot.

- Early aerial photographs were taken from hot air balloons.
- Cameras on satellites must be very advanced.
- Cameras on satellites are used to study everything from the earth's surface to weather patterns.

EYE IN THE SKY

In 1990, NASA launched the Hubble Space Telescope. On board was something called a Wide Field Planetary Camera. The images it sent back to Earth were fuzzy. A 1993 Space Shuttle *Endeavor* mission made needed repairs. A new Wide Field Planetary Camera was installed. The images sent since then have been breathtaking. Through Hubble's camera, people on Earth can see nebulas, star clusters, galaxies, and supernovas.

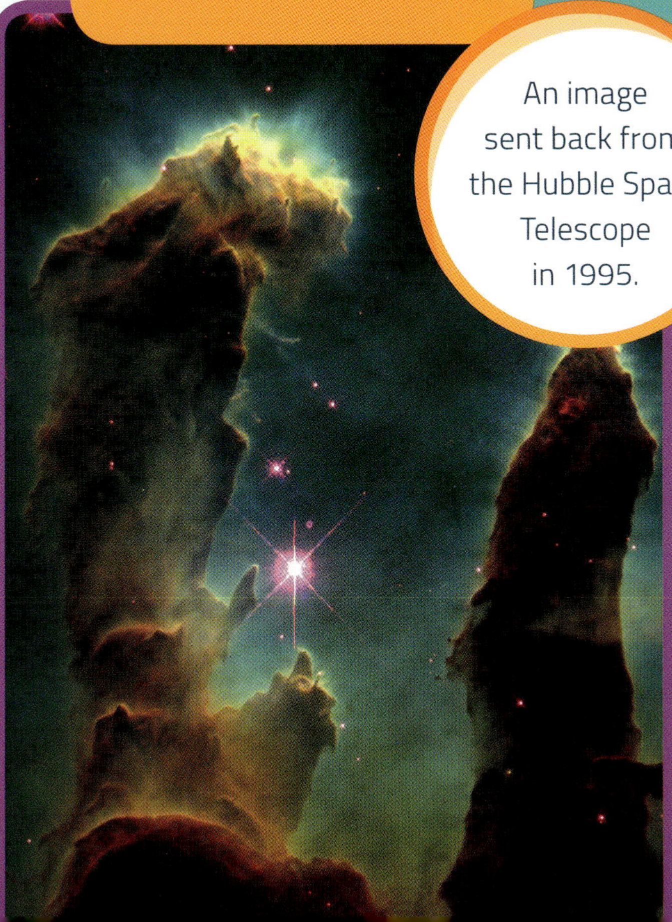

An image sent back from the Hubble Space Telescope in 1995.

world around us. Images from space make maps more accurate. They aid in predicting the weather and understanding Earth's changing climate.

Some satellites carry infrared or ultraviolet cameras. These cameras can see light that is not visible to human eyes. They allow astronomers to see faraway objects in space.

11

Cameras Keep Shrinking

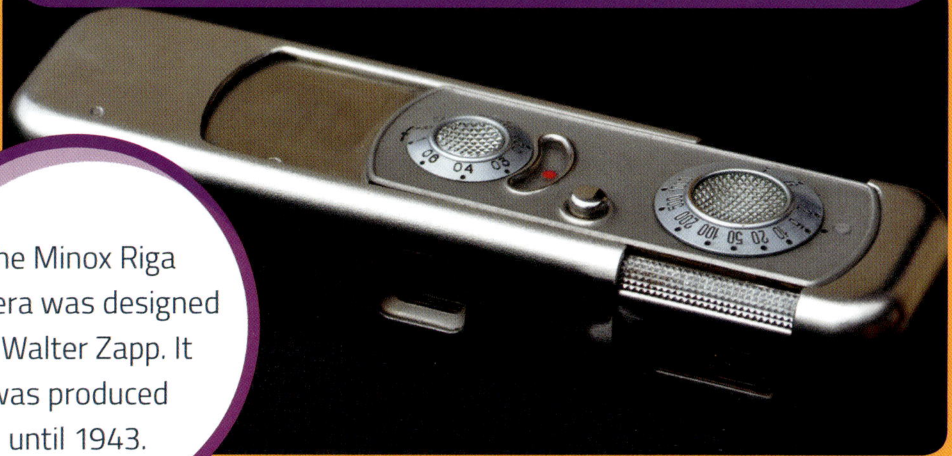

The Minox Riga camera was designed by Walter Zapp. It was produced until 1943.

Early cameras were big and bulky. It was hard to carry them around. Photographers needed to lug a lot of equipment to use them. But advances in technology have made cameras smaller and smaller.

One famous tiny camera was the Minox Riga from the late 1930s. It was about the size of a finger. It could take up to 50 photos. This camera was typically used by spies.

With the invention of digital photography, cameras kept getting smaller. Cameras are now almost everywhere. People have cameras in their smartphones and their cars. Doorbell cameras let people look at a smartphone or tablet to see who's at the door. Tiny cameras are used in factories and hospitals.

THINK ABOUT IT

Cameras today are small enough to be hidden almost anywhere. They are in phones and can be placed on drones. What problems might this cause for people's privacy?

In the early 2000s, drones started to become popular. Some of these flying devices can fit in the palm of a person's hand. They carry tiny cameras.

Some of the smallest cameras nowadays can sit on the tip of a person's finger. These cameras do not need memory chips to store images. They send images wirelessly to a user.

1938

Year the Minox Riga camera was first produced.

- The earliest cameras were big and boxy.
- Some tiny cameras today can fit on the tip of a person's finger.
- Tiny cameras are common in drones and smartphones.

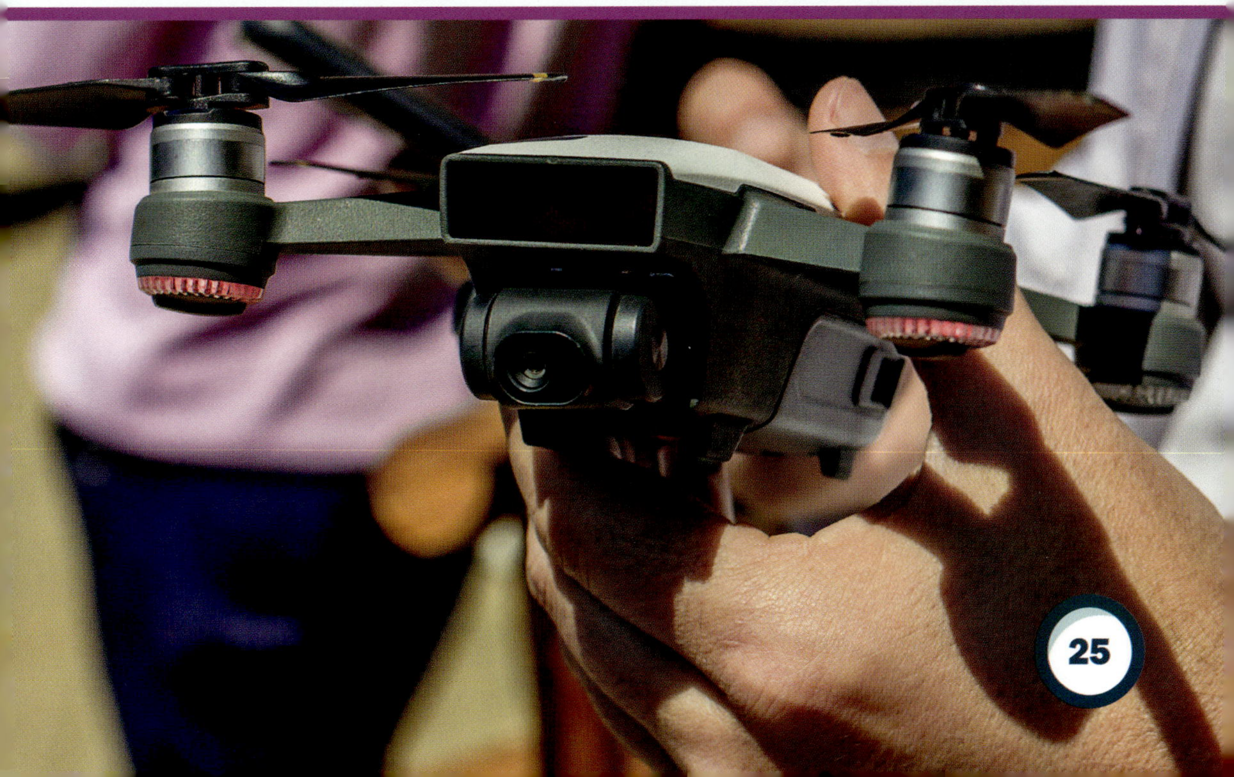

12

Photo Editing Fools the Eye

Changing a photograph in any way is called photo editing. Changes might include taking someone or something out of a picture. Or they might include adding someone or something. Photo editing can be used to fix problems and make photos look more professional.

Photo editing began almost as soon as people started taking photographs. Early attempts involved cutting and pasting negatives together. An image would be cut from one negative and added to another. Photographers sometimes did strange things to photographs. They would add a giant fish to a photograph. Or they might cut out a person's head and place it in their hands.

In the past, photo editing was done to clean up images. Drawing

1987

Year Adobe released its first version of a photo editing program called Photoshop.

- Photo editing is making any changes to a photograph.
- Early photo editing involved cutting and pasting negatives.
- Today people use software to edit digital photographs.

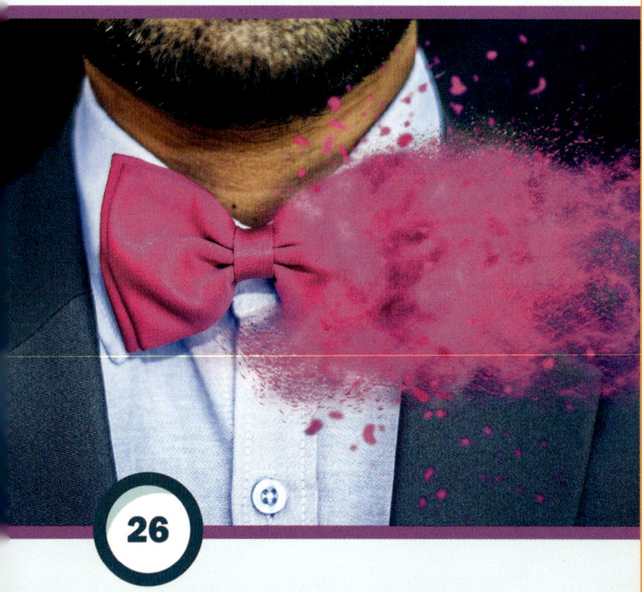

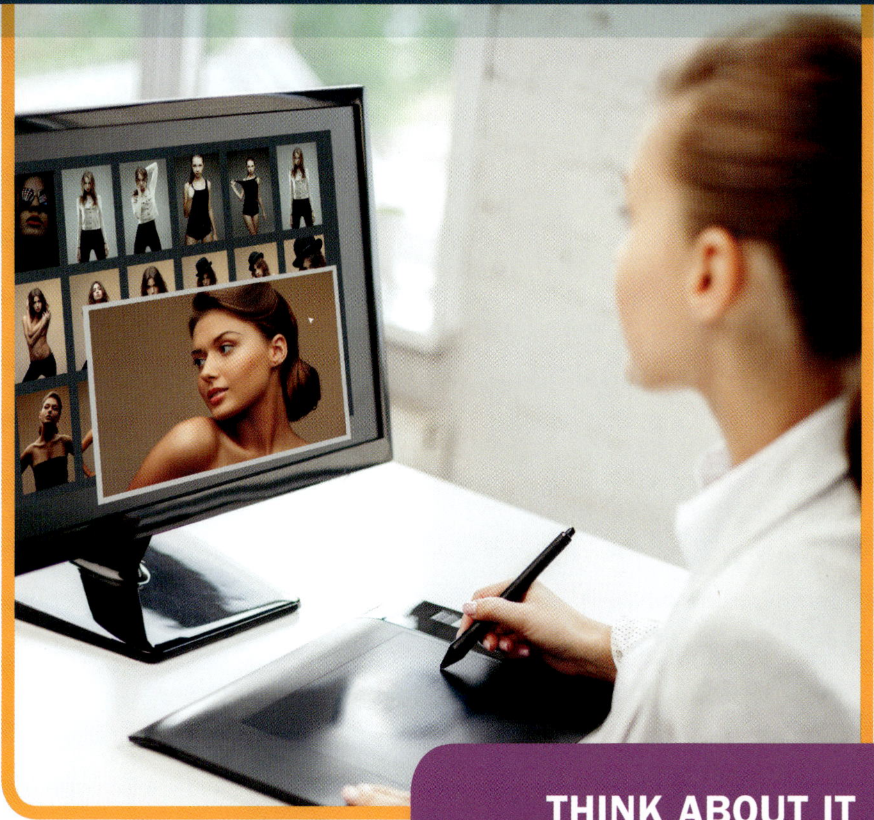

on negatives with ink would bring out certain details. Airbrushing smoothed wrinkles and erased blemishes. Some people colorized photographs by painting on negatives.

THINK ABOUT IT

What are your thoughts about people editing pictures of themselves they post online? Why might this be a good or a bad practice?

Today photo editing is much simpler. Because of digital photography, people no longer need to cut and paste negatives. With the right software and a few clicks, they can change anything. Any photo can be edited to create an outlandish or amazing picture.

Photo editing is also used to make people look perfect. Some young people see the photos and feel bad about themselves. Most of the images in magazines, in advertisements, and online aren't how people look in real life.

Fact Sheet

- People have known about the camera obscura's optical illusion for thousands of years. But ancient peoples didn't understand how it worked or why the image appeared upside down. Arab scholar Ibn al-Haytham was born in 965 CE in what is now southern Iraq. He was the first to figure out that light travels in a straight line. He wrote down his ideas in *The Book of Optics*.
- In 1923, American photographer Samuel Shlafrock invented the instant camera. This camera had a single compartment that would expose and develop a photograph. But it was not until 1948 that instant cameras were sold commercially. That year, Polaroid released its Model 95 Land Camera. This camera took and developed a photograph within minutes.

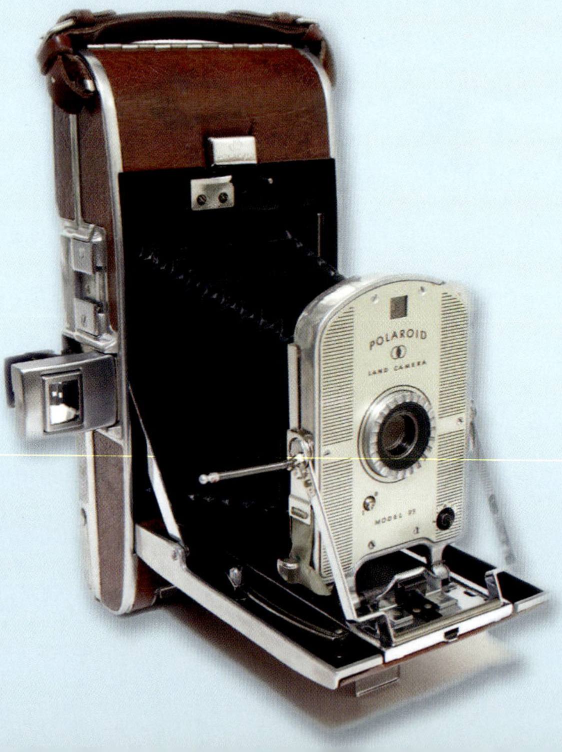

- George Eastman was one of the great innovators of modern photography. In 1892, he founded the Eastman Kodak Company. Eastman made cameras easier to use. He invented a machine that created dry photo plates. He developed flexible film and the process of having photographs professionally developed.

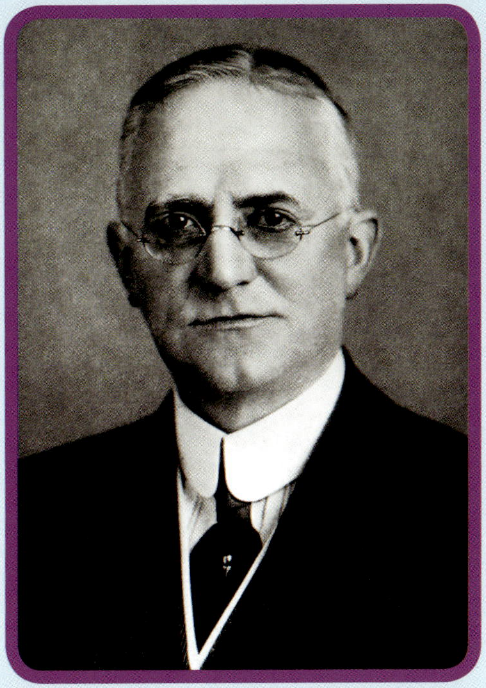

- Over the years, many types of spy cameras have been made. These are often small cameras that fool people into thinking they are something else. For example, some old spy cameras were built to look like lighters, watches, or pens.

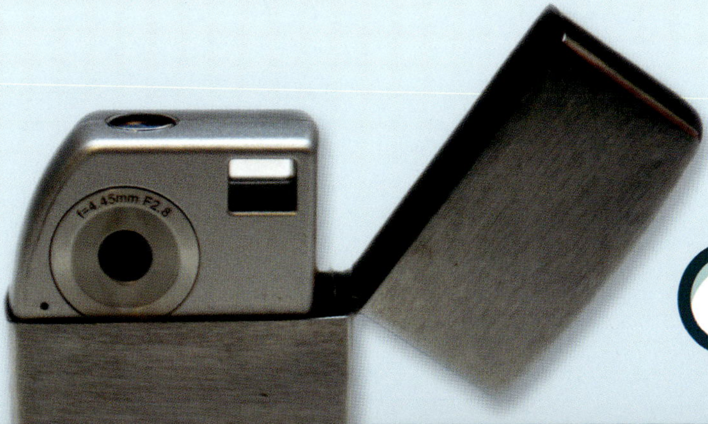

Glossary

aerial
Having to do with the air or sky.

astronomer
A person who studies objects in space.

chemical compound
Any mixing of two or more chemicals to produce another substance.

emulsion
A light-sensitive coating on photographic paper or film.

exposure
The amount of time light is allowed to shine on a plate, film, or sensor to make a photograph.

fixer
A chemical compound used to make sure an image doesn't fade away.

latent
Something that can't be seen.

Latin
The language of ancient Rome and the Roman empire.

negative
An image used to make a photograph. On a negative, dark areas appear light and light areas are dark.

optical illusion
Something that looks different than it actually is, such as a mirage.

photosensitive
Describes a surface or chemical that reacts to light.

sensor
A device that detects light, heat, sound, or movement and reacts in a certain way.

For More Information

Books

Oxlade, Chris. *Cameras*. Exploring Science. Helotes, TX: Armadillo Children's Publishing, 2016.

Spence, Kelly. *Maker Projects for Kids Who Love Photography*. New York: Crabtree Publishing Company, 2017.

Vallencourt, Margaret, Ed. *History of Photography*. New York: Britannica Educational Publishing in association with Rosen Educational Services, 2016.

Index

About the Author

Allan Morey grew up in central Wisconsin and now lives in St. Paul, Minnesota with his two dogs, Stitch and Ty. He has written more than 100 books for children, and especially enjoys writing about technology, sports, and space exploration.